PEDAL THE METAL

A History of Cars

By Jean Liccione

CELEBRATION PRESS
Pearson Learning Group

CONTENTS

People and Cars *3*

A Look Back *4*

Power *10*

Speed and Safety *13*

More Is Better *17*

Cars Go Wild! *23*

Cars of Today and Tomorrow *28*

Glossary *32*

Index .... *Inside Back Cover*

PEOPLE AND CARS

Many people today need a car in order to get around. If you live in a rural area or in a suburban neighborhood, you and your family probably need to drive when you shop, visit people, or go to school or work. In these areas, cars are a necessity.

Of course, not everyone needs a car. People who live in a city or in a small town may be able to walk most places. There may also be public transportation. People can ride a bus or subway to get where they want to go.

People who do have cars, though, often have personal feelings about them. Families may have nicknames for their cars. Some owners think of the car as part of their wardrobes. They may change cars just as they would change their clothes!

Some people love cars so much that they collect them. There are magazines and Web sites devoted to collectible cars—classic cars, oddball cars, and racing cars. Something about these cars makes them special.

What features distinguish one car from another? Cars can stand out because of their age, rarity, model, features, size, speed, or design. Let's take a look back to the time when cars were first invented—and *all* cars were viewed as unusual.

A LOOK BACK

In the 1800s, many people in Europe and America were trying to produce a vehicle with a motor that would not depend on animals for power. Some inventors used steam to power the engine. Others tried hot air, electricity, and even gunpowder.

The most successful of these early cars ran with steam or electricity. They were popular in the late 1800s and early 1900s. These "horseless carriages," as early cars were often called, weren't very practical. Think about having to boil water to get a car moving! That was how cars with steam engines were powered. The most successful steam car was the Stanley Steamer. Twin brothers Francis and Freelan

Twins Francis and Freelan Stanley in an early Stanley Steamer

Stanley built about 11,000 of their steam-powered cars between 1897 and 1922.

To start a Steamer, the driver had to light a match, ignite a gas or kerosene burner, and boil water to create steam. The burner hung below the boiler inside the car's frame. The driver then waited about 20 minutes for enough steam pressure to build up to run the car. Steam-powered cars couldn't compete with cars that had electric starters, which first appeared in 1912. The last steam cars were produced in the 1920s.

You may think that interest in electric power for cars is a modern idea. That isn't true. Very early carmakers experimented with electric power. By 1900, electric engines were more popular than steam or gasoline engines. Battery-powered cars were clean and quiet.

The main problem with electric cars in the past, as is still true today, was the life of the batteries. The cars could go only from 30 to 75 miles before the batteries needed to be recharged. Long trips in an electric car were difficult or impossible. By the mid-1920s, most carmakers had stopped producing battery-powered cars.

Gasoline was by far the most successful fuel tried by car inventors. By 1876 a German inventor, Nikolaus Otto, had built an engine powered by gas.

One of Otto's engineers, Gottlieb Daimler, put an engine of the type invented by Otto into a motor car in the mid-1880s. So did an inventor named Karl Benz. They began selling their cars in Europe. Then, inventors in other countries began to produce their own motor cars. In America, the brothers Charles and Frank Duryea formed the first car manufacturing company in 1895.

Early Cars Drive Fashion

Early cars were slow, dirty, and dangerous. Most had no enclosed space, so the driver and passengers were exposed to the open air. Clothing and fashions were developed for protection from the dust and for a well-dressed look. Both men and women wore full-length coats called dusters. Men also wore caps, whereas women wore hats with veils. The driver often wore goggles for eye protection.

Full-length coats, or "dusters," such as this one, were worn by both men and women.

Cars for Everyone

Car manufacturing was a slow process. For instance, in 1896, the Duryea Motor Wagon Company made only 13 cars. This meant the first cars were expensive. They also broke down often and were difficult to operate. For these reasons, they were owned mainly by wealthy people who could afford to hire a **chauffeur**.

In the United States, some early manufacturers such as Ransom E. Olds and Henry Ford found new ways to produce affordable cars. Olds introduced the idea of the **assembly line**. Standing in a line, each worker did part of the assembling job. In 1 year, the Olds Motor Works could turn out thousands of cars.

From 1908 to 1927, Henry Ford built several versions of his Model T car. To make the car, Ford improved on **mass-production** methods begun by Olds. He began using **conveyor belts** in his factory.

A family rides in an early version of Ford's Model T.

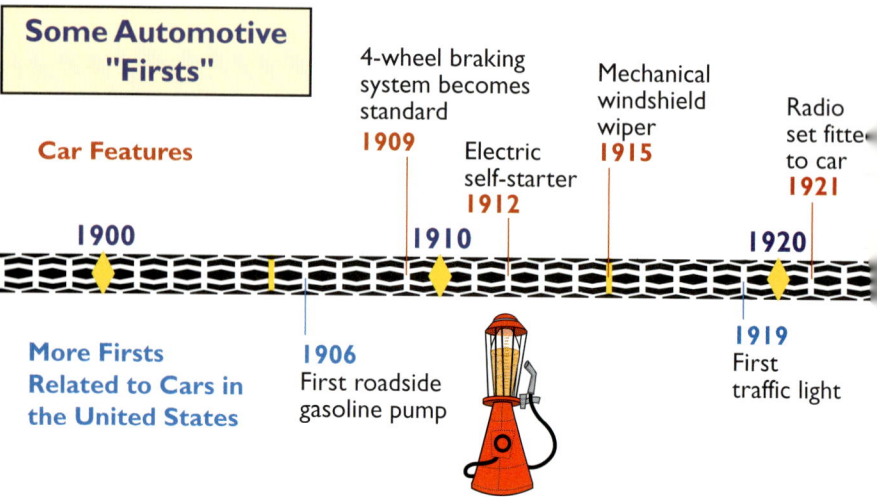

A long belt made of a strong material moved car parts from one worker to another.

Since Ford hardly ever changed the look of his Model T, he was able to buy large numbers of parts cheaply. Assembly lines helped his workers put cars together quickly. The result was a car that most families could afford. Ford's 1925 Model T, the Runabout, was probably the lowest-priced car ever produced. It cost $260.

Soon there were more car choices for the average buyer. Carmakers such as General Motors and Chrysler began building their own cars. GM sold more Chevrolets in 1927 than Ford sold Model Ts.

From 1900 to 1950, numerous improvements emerged. Manufacturers competed for customers with new car models and features. Many things we

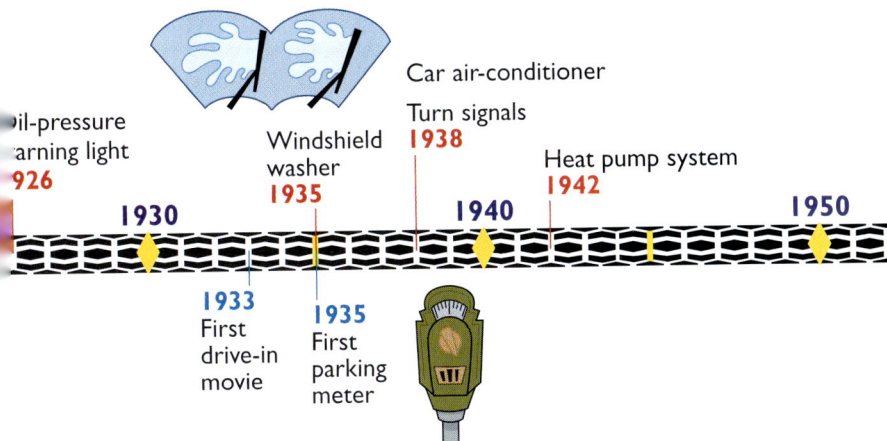

take for granted today, such as turn signals, were introduced in the first half of the twentieth century.

Production of cars halted in America during World War II. The factories were needed to produce planes, tanks, and motor vehicles to help fight the war. After the war ended in 1945, manufacturers went back to making cars.

As cars became widely available again, the American landscape changed. Motels, shopping malls, highways, and suburbs all developed along with the automobile. So did drive-in movies and drive-through windows at restaurants and banks.

Today, cars are produced all over the world, and millions of people own cars. In 1999, there were more than 130 million private and commercial automobiles owned in the United States.

9

POWER

As automobiles developed and changed in the twentieth century, their engines became more powerful. Why was this important? A car with a powerful engine can go very fast. It can also climb hills more easily than a car with a less powerful engine can. In addition, an engine's power controls how quickly a car can **accelerate**, or gain a desired speed. The phrase "zero to 60" describes how much time it takes for a car standing still to achieve the speed of 60 miles per hour. It is related to an engine's power.

A modern car is far more powerful than a horse. However, people still keep track of the power of a

The 1962 Chevrolet Impala SS 409 could go from 0 to 60 miles per hour in 7.3 seconds.

car's engine by referring to its **horsepower**. One unit of horsepower (hp) is equal to the force needed to raise 33,000 pounds 1 foot in 1 minute. In 1914, the engine of a Chevrolet Baby Grand touring car delivered about 22 hp. Compare that to the 1957 Cadillac Eldorado. Its engine delivered 300 hp!

The unit of measurement was first called horsepower by James Watt, who is known for his work on the steam engine. Watt discovered that a horse could raise 33,000 pounds of coal up a mine shaft at the rate of 1 foot per minute. One horsepower represents the ability of an engine to do the same amount of work in the same time.

Today, a car engine's power is often stated as brake horsepower, or bhp. This is the actual, or useful, horsepower of an engine. It takes into account the effects of friction and other power-losing forces affecting the engine.

Gasoline became the most popular fuel after the discovery of oil gushers in Texas in 1901. Today, nearly all cars run on a gasoline engine mounted at the front of the car.

It was the early carmaker Karl Benz who designed an engine with 4 **cylinders** and mechanical **valves**. Manufacturing companies have continued to use this basic design to this day, sometimes with 6, 8, or 12 cylinders.

These engines are called internal combustion engines. When the driver turns the key in the **ignition**, power flows from the car's battery to the starter. This sets the **pistons** inside the cylinders in motion. A piston moves up and down in a series of four strokes. The movement of the piston causes a mixture of air and gasoline to explode. The explosion produces power, which pushes the piston down. The motion of the piston turns the crankshaft and the gears of the transmission, providing the power needed to move the car. When the power of the turning gears is directed to the front wheels, the car has front-wheel drive. When the power is sent along a shaft to the rear wheels, the car has rear-wheel drive.

Four-Cylinder Engine

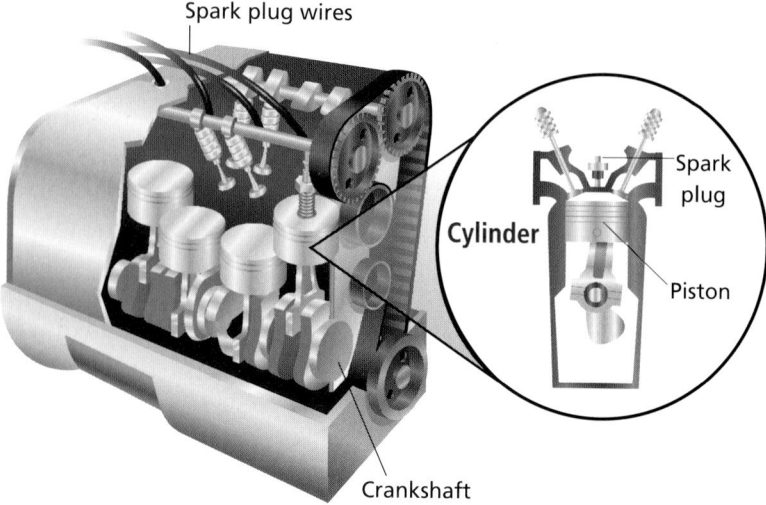

SPEED AND SAFETY

People have been racing cars ever since the automobile was invented. In the beginning, however, there were no special racing cars. Ordinary road cars were used for racing.

Sponsored car racing in the United States began in 1895. A newspaper, the *Chicago Times-Herald*, organized this road race. The course went from Chicago to Evanston, Illinois, and back. The race was won by a Duryea car, going an average of 7.5 miles per hour! Road races like this one were a common type of early car race. Drivers traveled on rough roads to see whose car could get from place to place fastest—and in one piece!

In 1906, a Stanley Steamer model, the Rocket, set a new land speed record of 127.66 miles per hour. In 1907, the Stanley brothers raced an even faster model. It went more than 150 miles per hour and broke apart. The driver went to the hospital, and the Stanley brothers gave up racing.

For some carmakers, winning a race was a form of advertising. William Durant had this idea in mind when he started the Chevrolet Motor Company. Durant hired a famous Swiss race driver, Louis Chevrolet, to design his cars.

Built for Speed

In the United States, closed-course racing on an oval track became popular. The famous track in Indianapolis, home of the Indy 500, was built in 1909. In 1911, the first 500-mile race was won there at an average speed of 74.59 miles per hour.

As car racing became more popular around the world, the design of race cars became highly specialized. Today, there are three basic types of race car. Formula One (F1) cars are single-seat racing cars that must meet specific standards in design and safety. They zoom around Grand Prix courses that have long straights and sharp hairpin turns. F1 cars reach average speeds of more than 200 miles per hour.

Indy cars are similar in design to F1 cars, with open cockpits and rear-mounted engines. They are slower

Formula One cars such as this one must meet specific standards in design and safety.

Stock cars look like typical cars on the outside. Jeff Gordon's car is in the lead position.

and heavier than F1 cars and more suited for oval track racing. In contrast, stock cars look more like typical cars. Under the **chassis**, though, stock cars are built for speed. The racing organization NASCAR oversees professional stock car racing, including the Winston Cup series.

These fast cars aren't the holders of the land speed record. To grab a land speed record today, a car does not usually follow strict racing design rules. Records are set by long runs at places such as the Bonneville Salt Flats in Utah. The engine of a land speed record-holder is probably a turbine, similar to a jet's engine.

Safety

Speed and safety on the road don't mix. As of 2001, motor vehicle accidents were the main cause of accidental death in the United States. More than 40,000 people are killed in traffic accidents every year, and more than 2 million are injured.

The quest for speed has led to some safety innovations. Some of those changes have come from the world of car racing.

For instance, early roads were a combination of dirt, mud, and rocks. The popularity of road races helped bring attention to the need for better roads. Accidents with racing cars showed the need for improved brakes and tires.

The roll bars on ordinary convertible cars were first developed for protection in open racing cars. Sturdier car frames, called roll cages, were first developed for closed racing cars. Seat belts and shoulder harnesses, first worn by racers, were required by law in American cars made as of 1968.

Other safety devices have been developed more recently to protect the average driver. Since 1998, car manufacturers have provided air bags on all new vehicles. A cloth bag inflates in less than 1 second after a collision. New braking systems also improve safety for drivers. Antilock brakes help the driver stay in control and steer the car if he or she has to brake quickly.

MORE IS BETTER

Some car owners just want a car to get them from place to place. Others are very competitive. These owners want their car to be something special. Manufacturers try to give customers what they want. An ad from Audi appeals to this feeling. It says, "Never think great is good enough. Never follow." For the past century, carmakers have tried to make cars that will please even the most demanding car buyers.

Luxury Cars

One of the most glamorous cars has always been the Rolls-Royce. Early ads appealed to an owner's sense of luxury. The only slogan the company used was "The Best Car in the World."

An advertisement for Rolls-Royce's Silver Cloud model

Rolls-Royce began with its famous Silver Ghost model of 1906 and continued the Silver name with the Silver Shadow, Silver Cloud, and Silver Spirit. The names were meant to suggest how quietly the cars ran. The Rolls-Royce was popular with maharajas, or princes, in India. They ordered custom-made cars and loaded them with gold, silver, and ivory. A Silver Ghost could cost about $10,000 when it was first made. Today, collectors will pay up to $500,000 for one! The base price of today's Rolls-Royce Silver Seraph is about $240,000.

Another car that symbolized luxury before World War II was the Packard. The company was known for the cars it custom-made for kings and queens. A special bullet-proof Packard was made in 1938 for President Franklin Delano Roosevelt.

Before World War II, the name *Packard* stood for luxury.

The Duesenberg was another outstanding luxury car of the 1920s and 1930s. Only about 500 were built between 1928 and 1938. With a powerful engine, the Duesenberg was as fast as it was elegant-looking. At a time when a worker might make $20 a week, a Duesenberg might cost from $14,000 to $25,000 or more. The saying "It's a Doozy" comes from the Duesenberg car. It means that something is outstanding.

After World War II, the Cadillac became a symbol of glamour and luxury. Stars such as Elvis Presley owned them. (Elvis's was pink.) A Cadillac figured in the plot of the 1956 movie *The Solid Gold Cadillac*.

Postwar manufacturers gave car buyers more than luxury. Sports cars gave ordinary car buyers the chance to drive cars that could reach high speeds. During the 1960s, Ford's Cobra was marketed as a speedy sports car. In this group, too, were the Alfa Romeo Spider, the Chevrolet Corvette, and the Ferrari.

Cars with high-performing, high-horsepower engines were nicknamed muscle cars. The production of muscle cars began in the 1960s. The Pontiac GTO was one of the earliest. It had a big engine in a mid-sized body. The Ford Mustang, introduced in 1964, was another small car with a muscular engine. Muscle cars lost their popularity in the 1970s as carmakers began making cars that were more fuel efficient.

Cars That Climb Mountains

Sports utility vehicles, or SUVs, are one of the latest styles of car to satisfy a driver's desire for "more." The SUV is like a modern version of the station wagon. With a light truck frame and a roomy interior, it is designed to carry anything. An SUV is also built to perform well under regular driving conditions as well as on very rough roads.

One example of an SUV that can be driven over rough terrain is the 2003 Hummer H2 from General Motors. A news release for the Hummer H2 said that the model could travel through streams 20 inches deep and climb 16-inch steps and rocks. Customers are willing to pay more for a vehicle that can do those things.

The Hummer H2 SUV is designed for rough terrain.

The *Thrust SSC* set the land speed record in 1997.

The Biggest and the Best
Here are some fun facts about record-holders that show people's desire for "more" from their cars:

- The most expensive car on record is a 1931 Bugatti Type 41 Royale. It was sold in 1990 for $15 million.

- The widest cars ever made were the 1961 and 1968 Chrysler Imperials. Both were nearly 7 feet wide.

- The longest car in the world is a 26-wheel custom limousine. It is 100 feet long and has a swimming pool complete with diving board!

- The fastest land speed record was set by a car called the *Thrust SSC*. It broke the sound barrier and set the land speed record in 1997, reaching a top speed of 763.03 miles per hour.

What's in a Name?

The names of some early cars may seem unusual to us. Did you ever hear of the Auto Red Bug, the Pup, the Bugmobile, or the Seven Little Buffaloes? How about the Allen, the Bantam, or the Chicago Electric? If you went through the letters of the alphabet, you could find a car name for almost every letter. These, and many other kinds of cars and their makers, came and went with almost no one knowing their names.

Many early cars, such as Fords, Duesenbergs, and Packards, were named for their makers. In time, car names became more original. Some carmakers named their cars for famous explorers. The Cadillac, DeSoto, and LaSalle are all in this group.

Other cars were named after animals to show strength and speed. Model names such as Mustang, Cougar, and Jaguar suggest the buyer is getting something fast and strong.

Some car names are just fanciful. The Lotus, for instance, is named for the lotus flower, whereas the Mercury is named for the planet. The Excalibur gets its name from the legendary King Arthur's sword. Other car names are supposed to suggest the character of the car. Car names that fall into this category include the Rover, the Power, and the Valiant.

What would you name a car? What characteristics do you think appeal to people today?

CARS GO WILD!

Carmakers have always tried new and different attractions to lure buyers. Some of these car features, such as turn signals, are so useful that it's hard to imagine a time when they were not available.

New and Unusual

Not all the changes, however, have been successful. One example is the Octoauto, introduced by the Reeves Company in 1911. It had four wheel axles and eight wheels. Steering was nearly impossible, and only one Octoauto was made. The Reeves Company also made a six-wheeler, but that didn't catch on either.

Manufacturers experimented with different numbers of wheels. This Octoauto had eight!

In America during the 1950s, speed and style sold cars. New features, such as the automatic transmission, were important. Before automatic transmissions, drivers had to step on a clutch pedal and shift gears by hand to go faster or slower. Now the car could shift the gears automatically.

Carmakers' ads of the 1950s sent the message that owning one of the manufacturer's new models would make the buyer more glamorous. Station wagons, convertibles, sports cars, and sedans all went wild! Most American cars of the late 1950s had large tail fins, fabulous hood ornaments, two-tone paint, and chrome. The 1959 Cadillac Eldorado had huge fins. Weighing about 2 tons, it was nearly 20 feet long. It only got 8 miles to the gallon, but fuel was cheap!

The tail fins on the 1959 Cadillac Eldorado were shaped like rockets.

At the other end of the car size range was the Fiat 500, introduced in Italy in 1957. This tiny car had an engine mounted at the back. It got more than 52 miles per gallon. About 4 million Fiats were built over the next 20 years. Another very small car was called the Mini.

The year 1957 also saw the beginning of a spectacular failure: the Edsel. It was made by the Ford Motor Company and named for a son of Henry Ford. The unusual front grille was described by one person as looking like "an Oldsmobile sucking a lemon." The company predicted it would sell 200,000 Edsels the first season, yet it sold only 62,000. The Edsel was dumped after being in production for only 2 years. People just didn't like its looks. Over time, the name *Edsel* became a symbol of a classic marketing failure.

The prize for production of one model goes to the Volkswagen Beetle. The VW Beetle was first manufactured in Germany in 1938. It became a huge hit in the United States starting in the late 1950s. More than 21 million have been made.

The Beetle became the world's best-selling model. It even beat the Ford Model T, of which 15 million were made. The original Beetle is still manufactured in Mexico today, and a "New Beetle" was introduced in the United States in 1998.

Cars for the Movies

Some cars become classics after they "star" in a movie or on television. In *The Love Bug*, made in 1969, a Volkswagen Beetle named Herbie was the star. In several James Bond movies, an Aston Martin DB5 was fitted with gimmicks such as an ejector seat. Fantasy cars such as Bond's Aston Martin are common status symbols for today's movie heroes.

Custom Cars

People have been customizing their cars since the days of the first luxury cars. Customizing a car can mean anything from doing a simple paint job to adding traffic-stopping designs to reshaping the chassis. It allows the owner to make an unusual car from an ordinary one.

With a custom car, the rule is "anything goes."

Newly styled headlights, taillights, hubcaps, interior upholstery, and paint colors and patterns turn cars into art. Some owners who are talented mechanics change their cars' engines to make them more powerful. These are known as hot rod engines.

In the 1950s, customizing cars was so popular that owners helped invent the practice of "cruising." Driving up and down the street was a way to show off their one-of-a-kind cars. Today, cruising is popular again. Wild custom cars will never go out of style.

Advertisers also make custom cars. By adding their own decorations, they can grab customers' attention. One popular hot dog company added a huge frankfurter to the roof of a car. It was quite a sight!

Some customized cars have features that take them to new places. The Aerocar, with detachable wings and tail, can fly! Its inventor made only five Aerocars, and one is still in use. The owner can drive to the airport, then take off. Inventors have also made vehicles that are half-car and half-boat. One of these, the Amphicar, was mass-produced in the 1960s. Some Amphicars are still used today.

New custom cars are also made for today's wealthy customers. Standard car bodies can be made longer. They can also be fitted with luxuries such as custom woodwork, crystal light fixtures, heated leather seats, color televisions, telephones, and computers.

CARS OF TODAY AND TOMORROW

Today's cars would amaze early manufacturers. Travel by automobile has become safer and more entertaining than it was a century ago. Modern cars are also built to meet environmental standards.

New Systems

Do you use maps to get where you want to go? With a navigation system in the car, a computer gives the directions. Navigation systems use global positioning signals from satellites. When the driver indicates a destination, the navigation system plots the best route and shows it on a screen. Some will even talk to you!

Car entertainment systems can make a long trip seem as if you're sitting at home. Some models come with screens for television, video or DVD, and computer games. Ask your grandparents what they did on a long car trip for entertainment. Then compare that with what is possible today!

If you are likely to lose your car keys, a keyless entry and ignition system may be the solution. In 1999, the Mercedes-Benz S-Class model introduced this feature. With a plastic card, programmed with a code, the door unlocks as you move toward the car. To start the engine, the driver then presses a button.

Fuel Efficiency

Gas became a common fuel worldwide after the discovery of great quantities of oil. Early cars, with heavy bodies, got low **fuel efficiency**. Because gasoline was cheap, no one seemed to mind. However, in the mid-1970s, the oil-producing countries of the Middle East slowed production. Long lines formed at gas stations in the United States.

Now people wanted cars that got higher fuel efficiency. The size of the engine in a car helps determine fuel efficiency. A large, powerful engine gives faster acceleration and better power for climbing hills. However, the buyer will pay more for gasoline because the car will use up fuel faster.

During the 1970s, fuel shortages meant long lines at the gas pump.

Today, the U.S. government sets fuel efficiency standards. The higher the fuel efficiency, the more miles a car gets per gallon of gasoline. In 1974, passenger cars averaged 14 miles per gallon. By 1985, the standard had been set at 27.5 miles per gallon. Carmakers have partially avoided these standards. Classified as light trucks, SUVs and minivans are required to get only 20.7 miles per gallon.

Keeping the Environment Clean

Tailpipe **emissions** produce particles that form smog and pollute the air. The governor of California signed a bill in 2002 requiring lower emissions for cars and light trucks. Cars with a 2009 model year and beyond will have to meet the new standards.

Toyota and Honda have cars with hybrid engines. *Hybrid* means the cars use both gasoline and electricity. They generate their own electricity, so they don't need to be plugged in to recharge the batteries. Because they run part of the time on battery power, they get better fuel efficiency when they do run on gasoline. The Honda Insight, a gasoline-electric hybrid, gets about 61 miles per gallon when driven in a city.

Carmakers continue to experiment with power sources. Steam or electric cars could make a comeback. Solar batteries might also power cars someday.

Concept Cars

Modern car designers use CAD programs, or computer-aided design. These programs allow engineers to design new car bodies and features, try them out, and then make changes right away on the screen.

Manufacturers today spend millions of dollars on style and engineering. They use designs to make prototypes called concept cars. These are working models of cars that a company may sell in the future. Some concept cars end up in the junkyard or in storage. Others are displayed in museums or at car shows. In 2002, Ford decided to sell some of its concept cars.

When you are ready to buy or drive a car, there will be even more choices than there are today. Perhaps you will become a collector of one of those unusual cars of the past—or of the future!

Cadillac's Cien, a two-seat sports car, is a concept car.

GLOSSARY

accelerate — to gain speed

assembly line — a line of factory workers and equipment in which a product such as a car is put together, step by step

chassis — the frame that supports the body of a car

chauffeur — a person hired as the driver of a car

conveyor belts — bands of strong, flexible material that move continuously to transport items from one place to another

cylinders — the engine parts that hold the pistons

emissions — fumes and particles given off when gasoline is burned for fuel

fuel efficiency — the measure of an engine's ability to consume fuel with the least waste

horsepower — a unit used to measure the power of a motor or engine, equal to the power needed to lift 33,000 pounds 1 foot per minute

ignition — the electrical system that sets fire to the fuel in a gasoline engine

mass production — making something in large amounts, usually using machinery

pistons — the engine parts that move up and down by pressure of gas or steam

valves — the engine parts that control the flow of air and gasoline into the cylinders